# GB RAILFREIGHT

## John Jackson

AMBERLEY

First published 2020

Amberley Publishing
The Hill, Stroud
Gloucestershire, GL5 4EP

www.amberley-books.com

Copyright © John Jackson, 2020

The right of John Jackson to be identified as
the Author of this work has been asserted in
accordance with the Copyrights, Designs and
Patents Act 1988.

ISBN 978 1 4456 8211 2 (print)
ISBN 978 1 4456 8212 9 (ebook)

British Library Cataloguing in Publication Data.
A catalogue record for this book is available from
the British Library.

Origination by Amberley Publishing.
Printed in the UK.

# Contents

# Introduction

I enjoy following a 'man with a mission'. In an ever-changing commercial world, it is always a pleasure to witness a success story in the making. That's particularly true of any player in the railway industry of today and even more so if that company was born after our railways entered the privatised era.

In the rail freight sector, two private companies had emerged from the ashes of British Rail's freight business during the transition from a nationalised to a privatised railway in the mid-1990s. They were to become DB Cargo (known as EWS around that time) and Freightliner. Since then, we've also seen Direct Rail Services (DRS) and Colas Rail operating in the UK freight sector. For me, however, without a shadow of doubt, the success story of the last two decades has been the growth of GB Railfreight, with Managing Director John Smith at the helm.

I can only speculate as to Mr Smith's exact 'mission' when starting the business but what has been created over the last twenty years is unparalleled in the UK rail industry.

It's not easy to keep pace with the exact figures as the company's growth continues. Today, the company prides itself on customer service, with a reliability level of around 99 per cent. This is achieved by making the welfare of the 1,000 or so members of its staff team a top priority. As I spend hundreds of hours every year observing the rail industry at work, I feel qualified to say that the staff's professionalism and focus on the customer is there for all to see.

In this book we focus on the trains themselves. With a fleet of over 150 locos, GBRf now operates around 1,500 trainloads in a typical week.

Let's briefly turn the clock back twenty years to the company's beginnings.

GB Railfreight was founded in 1999 by John Smith, a career railwayman working latterly as MD on Anglia Railways. GBRf became part of the First Group early in the twenty-first century and then, in 2010, it became part of the Eurotunnel's rail freight subsidiary, Europorte. Six years later, the company was sold again. From 2016 until autumn 2019, GBRf has been in the hands of Swedish private equity group EQT, through its subsidiary Hector Rail. As I complete this introduction, however, news of the company's sale from Hector Rail to Infracapital is hot off the press.

Infracapital is the unlisted infrastructure equity arm of M&G Prudential. Their joint press release boasts that GBRf now accounts for 23 per cent of the UK's total rail cargo, and the estimated 2019 turnover for GBRf is £200 million. The deal is scheduled for October 2019 so, as they say, watch this space!

As well as the company's core rail freight business, ten years ago it was granted a licence to operate passenger services in the UK, with the Caledonian Sleeper service between London and Scotland probably the best known. The company's Class 73 and Class 92 locos are both used on these services.

The company has, more recently, won contracts for delivery and movement of other operators' rolling stock, such as the Siemens-built Class 700 units and Class 800 IEP trains from Hitachi.

In 2000, the newly formed company secured a contract to operate infrastructure trains for Railtrack. By that time both major freight operators, EWS and Freightliner, had taken delivery of their first examples of General Motors' Class 66 locomotives. On the strength of securing that lengthy Railtrack contract, GBRf ordered seven similar locos for its own use. Their numbers ranged from 66701 to 66707, with the locos built in early 2001 and delivered shortly after.

My trusty notebook reveals that my own first encounter with the company's new locos was on 22 June 2001 at Peterborough. No. 66702 was to be found stabled in the company yard there, with sister loco No. 66701 making an appearance through the station on a northbound rake of Railtrack-branded hoppers the same day. My photo of this working appears at the front of the book, and, appropriately, the loco was already carrying the name *Railtrack National Logistics*.

Perhaps just as significant was the commencement of GBRf intermodal services the following year. The company is, of course, now a major player in the movement of containerised goods in the UK. Its first service began running in February 2002 from the Port of Felixstowe to the freight terminal at Hams Hall in the West Midlands. The service was operated for Medite Shipping Company (MSC) and the working remains in the weekday timetable today. The growth in GBRf's container traffic and its importance as a major player in the sector was again underlined in the autumn of 2019. The company has just announced the introduction of its seventeenth intermodal service operating from Southampton to Trafford Park, Manchester. This new service represents the third GBRf daily working from the South Coast port.

The company's operations have continued to diversify since those early years, with contracts secured including the movement of gypsum, coal and, later, biomass. To keep pace with this growth in customers, the fleet of Class 66s has continuously expanded with it. Business growth in the South East of England led the company into use of redundant Class 73 electro-diesels, which were more appropriate to the third rail area, and would probably have been described as bi-mode in today's railway parlance.

The company has been continually on the lookout, both near and far, to meet its demand for an ever-increasing number of Class 66 diesel locos. The fleet has expanded with locos procured from both mainland Europe and other UK operators. Direct Rail Services, Freightliner, Colas Rail and DB Cargo have all contributed to GBRf's Class 66 fleet.

Worthy of mention is the company's loco naming policy which now has the majority of Class 66s suitably adorned. Names carried vary from football clubs (the MD is a fanatical Sunderland supporter) to a variety of railway companies and individuals who have contributed to rail history. Key customers are also included as are various members of the company's staff. Most are, of course, planned but one exception was that of No. 66732's naming in 2009. The MD seemed totally surprised at the inclusion of his own name when the nameplate was revealed as *GBRf The First Decade 1999–2009 John Smith – MD.*

In an earlier publication for Amberley Publishing, *Nameplates –The Story Behind the Names,* the background behind a number of GBRf loco namings was included. Space here does not enable me to go into further details on the remainder. Suffice it to say that most, if not all, are pertinent to the company, its staff, its customers and the railway sector as a whole.

As I write these notes, the operational Class 66 fleet stands at eighty-eight in traffic (numbered 66701–66733, 66735–66789). A further three, Nos 66790–66792, are in the process of being added to the fleet, with the first two of these having recently arrived at Electromotive's depot in Longport, near Stoke-on-Trent.

The 'missing' No. 66734 is included in the pages that follow, although it was scrapped following an accident in 2012. Railway accidents are, thankfully, extremely rare and I am happy to report the driver was unhurt following the loco's derailment near Tulloch on Scotland's West Highland Line. The working was a rake of Alcan tanks between Blyth and Fort William. The loco was less fortunate, having come to rest close to the shore of Loch Treig. It was later cut up on site. By an ironic twist, the Gaelic translation of Loch Treig is 'Loch of Death'.

The fleet of Class 66s is supported by twenty-four Class 73 locomotives (of which four are stored) and sixteen Class 92s (twelve operational and four stored). The company fleet operates a variety of other locomotive classes, notably eight veteran Class 20s, a single Class 59, No. 59003 (brought back from Germany in 2014) and ten Class 60s acquired from Colas Rail in 2018. The Class 20s were primarily used on the recently completed contract to move stock on behalf of London Underground Limited.

The fleet is augmented by a small pool of other locomotives of Classes 47, 50 and 56. Finally, in addition to the expanding loco fleet, the company operates a pool of more than 1,000 wagons. We take a look at a few examples of these towards the end of this publication.

In this publication, I have included a wide range of locos, representing almost all of the company's fleet, performing a variety of workings. This includes all eighty-nine examples of the company's Class 66s at work.

I hope the reader will agree that these photos are a testament to the GBRf success story, with their business spread across a variety of goods and services and extending to most corners of the UK. The freight sector, as a whole, has seen a dramatic downturn in traffic such as coal and steel in recent years. GBRf has, however, risen to this challenge and has enjoyed expansion of its activities in other areas such as the construction and aggregates business, in particular. Finally, the views in this publication are my own, and, in my view, GB Railfreight deserves to flourish!

As always, I hope you enjoy your journey through the pages that follow as much as I have enjoyed compiling them.

John Jackson

# GB Railfreight – Then and Now

## GB Railfreight – Then (2001)

This photo was taken on 22 June 2001, not long after the company had taken delivery of its first batch of Class 66 locomotives. First numbered 66701, then appropriately named *Railtrack National Logistics*, this loco is seen heading north through Peterborough on a rake of Railtrack-branded infrastructure wagons. It was the securing of this Railtrack contract that set GB Railfreight on its way.

## GB Railfreight – Now (2019)

Almost twenty years later and the fleet of GBRf's Class 66 locomotives now numbers around ninety, with No. 66789 *British Rail 1948–1997* the highest numbered in traffic at the time of writing. It is seen on 20 June 2019 heading south through Doncaster on a recently introduced service from Tees Dock. Despite the name it carries, no Class 66 locos have ever been owned by British Rail, with the entire class introduced in the privatised era.

## Class 20 Locomotives

GBRf has a small fleet of veteran English Electric Type 1 (Class 20) locomotives at its disposal. The fleet includes No. 20096, which was built in October 1961. It is seen here on 20 March 2013 at Burton-on-Trent in the company of sister loco No. 20107.

Class 20 No. 20107 is another 1961 veteran, built in December that year. On 15 November 2016 it is seen stabled at Derby in readiness for working from the nearby Litchurch Lane workshops.

Two years earlier, on 15 December 2014, No. 20118 *Saltburn-by-the-Sea* is stabled in almost the same place. In addition to its North East England nameplate, it also sports the kingfisher vinyls of one of its former depots, Thornaby, once one of the North East's largest loco bases.

Most of the work for this fleet of eight locos involved moving stock for London Underground Limited (LUL). These moves consisted of four locos, with a pair at each end, a couple of barrier wagons and the Underground trainset. On 2 March 2016, No. 20132 is seen at Leicester on a typical working from Old Dalby to LUL's depot at West Ruislip. Old Dalby, in Leicestershire, is the operations centre for a testbed line, running some 13 miles, on which new stock can be put through its paces prior to delivery.

On 13 October 2014, No. 20311 is involved in a very different working. Along with No. 20314, it was used to move No. 59003 from Immingham Docks on the loco's return to the UK (see later in this publication). The loco trio are seen passing Chesterfield.

Along with a number of other Class 20 locomotives, No. 20314 is owned by Harry Needle Railroad Company, and was subsequently hired to GBRf. On 5 July 2013, the loco waits at Leicester looking resplendent in its HN Rail colours.

Two of Harry Needle's Class 20s were given GBRf liveries. On 15 October 2015, No. 20901 stands at Derby waiting to take the barrier wagons into the works.

On 15 November 2016, sister loco No. 20905 stands in Derby on a similar move. The colourful combination is completed by, from left to right, Nos 20096, 20107 and 20314. The LUL contract was completed in June 2019, leaving us guessing as to what the future holds for these eight locomotives.

## Class 47 Locomotives

In 2017, GBRf bought three Class 47s from Colas Rail. These included No. 47727 *Edinburgh Castle*, which appeared in Caledonian Sleeper livery shortly afterwards. It is seen at Leicester on 6 September 2019.

Sister loco No. 47739 is also seen on Leicester depot. On 30 August 2019, it stands in the depot area sporting its GBRf house colours.

The third acquisition was No. 47749 *City of Truro*. It is seen at Peterborough depot on 25 April 2018, still in Colas Rail livery.

By the time this photo was taken on 16 June 2019, No. 47749 had been repainted in BR blue, with the Rail Services logo on its cabsides. It is approaching Nuneaton on a light engine move from Leicester to Long Marston.

## Class 50 Locomotives

GBRf also has two Class 50s now carrying its colours. In conjunction with the Class 50 Alliance, these two locos are available on an ad hoc basis for charters and heritage railway events, for example. Loco No. 50007, with sister No. 50049, stands at Eastleigh on 20 March 2019 waiting to run light engine to London, in readiness to work a charter to the West Country.

No. 50049 had earlier appeared from Eastleigh's workshops. It is seen in the station platform on a circular move via Romsey.

# Class 56 Locomotives

GBRf's ongoing quest for additional loco power saw its focus turn to a total of sixteen Class 56s from UK Rail Leasing. A selection of these acquisitions is seen on the next few pages, starting with this photo of No. 56031. On 3 December 2013, the loco is seen arriving at Leicester, still sporting the Fertis livery from its days on hire in France. It would spend the next five years or so within the area of the former Leicester depot.

These Class 56 acquisitions are a mix of serviceable and stored locos, including possible parts donors. None are yet in GBRf colours or service. Looking particularly forlorn, No. 56032 is seen on 31 July 2019 at Electromotive's plant at Longport, near Stoke-on-Trent. Class 66 No. 66726 is on the right.

No. 56037 stands in the foreground in this view of several Class 56s in the yard at Leicester on 4 June 2018. It is still sporting faded EWS colours.

Loco No. 56069 looks even more forlorn in this general view of Electromotive's yard at Longport on 31 July 2019. It is in the centre of this photo minus its cab windows.

Two of GBRf's Class 56 locos have been used for shunting moves in the Peak Forest area of Derbyshire. On 31 March 2019, No. 56081 is stabled there between duties.

The second loco, No. 56098, is seen hard at work the following day. It is involved in shunting wagons during the loading process at the nearby quarry at Dove Holes. Early in 2019, GBRf took over a number of workings from this important freight customer, with its Class 66 locos delivering to various locations across the country.

The former DC Rail-operated No. 56311 has also now moved to Longport. It still carries the DC Rail livery when seen at Leicester on 10 April 2018, prior to its move.

Sister DC Rail loco No. 56312 remains at Leicester. It is seen here, with its former nameplates obviously removed, during a shunting move at the depot on 26 April 2018. Conversion of at least one loco from this pool of Class 56s is expected, with a new Class 69 being envisaged.

# Class 59 Locomotive

GBRf's quest for yet more motive power led to the return of No. 59003 *Yeoman Highlander* after spending thirteen years in Germany. It returned to the UK via Immingham Docks. On 13 October 2014, it is seen passing Derby whilst being moved from Humberside to Eastleigh by Nos 20311 and 20314.

With its nameplates retained, No. 59003 now sports the GBRf house colours. On 16 July 2018, it is about to leave Eastleigh stabling point for its next duty.

## Class 60 Locomotives

A total of ten Colas Rail Class 60s were transferred to GBRf in the 2018 move, namely Nos 60002, 60021, 60026, 60047, 60056, 60076, 60085, 60087, 60095 and 60096. On 4 April 2019, No. 60021, still in Colas Rail livery, heads through Rainhill, Merseyside, on a Drax to Liverpool empty biomass working.

GBRf livery has just started to appear on these Class 60 locos. No. 60021 is seen alongside No. 73967 at Doncaster on 5 July 2019, sporting its new operator's colours. Its former *Bustler* nameplates have also been removed.

The swapping of locos on this Liverpool biomass traffic requires a light engine move to and from Doncaster depot. On 14 March 2019, No. 60076 is on the rear of such a convoy as it passes Doncaster station. Class 66 No. 66754 is leading with No. 60021 also in the consist.

On 29 June 2017, No. 60095, with Nos 60096 and 60045 for company, is seen at Doncaster on a light engine move from Barnetby to Toton. At the time of the photo there was much speculation that GBRf was interested in these machines. A year later and all three were to be in GBRf's loco fleet.

## Class 66 Locomotives

No. 66701, the pioneer Class 66 for GBRf, has been in traffic for almost twenty years. On 5 April 2018, the loco, currently unnamed, is seen passing Acton Yard, in West London, on a return working of empty hoppers from Colnbrook, near Heathrow, to Bardon Hill Quarry in Leicestershire.

All the major rail-based freight operators, including GBRf, have been exposed to the significant downturn in coal movements in recent years. On 3 October 2017, No. 66702 *Blue Lightning* passes Floriston crossing, north of Carlisle. It is on a loaded working from Kier Mining's surface mine at Greenburn, Ayrshire, to Drax power station in Yorkshire.

It is almost twenty years since GBRF started operating intermodal container trains, including from the UK's largest container port at Felixstowe. On 28 August 2018, No. 66703 *Doncaster PSB 1981–2002* heads south through Bletchley on a working from Trafford Park, near Manchester, to the Suffolk port.

GBRf is the haulier for Petrochem Carless's North Sea gas condensate traffic in East Anglia for that company's refinery in Harwich. At least once a week the empty tanks are taken to North Walsham, between Norwich and Cromer, for loading. On 8 July 2015, No. 66704 *Colchester Power Signalbox* hauls the loaded wagons through Ipswich station's centre road heading for Harwich.

No. 66705 *Golden Jubilee* is one of the original batch of seven Class 66 locos delivered back in 2001. It was named a year later to mark the Queen's fifty years since accession to the throne. The loco also sported a large Union Jack on its bodyside when this photo was taken at Stafford on 23 October 2012.

GBRf operated a number of trains in connection with the Crossrail project. They included spoil workings between Willesden and Barrington, near Foxton, in Cambridgeshire. On 8 July 2015, No. 66706 *Nene Valley* is seen waiting at Cambridge on the London-bound return working.

The yards at Toton, on the border between Nottinghamshire and Derbyshire, are better known as a major hub of competitor DB Cargo. An increasing number of GBRf workings now use the yards here as well as the through lines in the centre. On 21 October 2018, No. 66707 *Sir Sam Fay Great Central Railway* is seen in the yard at the head of an unidentified engineers' working.

As the company's business expanded, further Class 66 locos were ordered, with No. 66708 *Jayne* arriving in 2002. On 7 August 2019 it is seen heading north through Chesterfield on an intermodal service. This time the working is from the Port of Southampton to the iPort rail terminal at Rossington, near Doncaster.

Chesterfield is, again, the location in this photo taken on 29 January 2019. This time the GBRf working is for the Ministry of Defence, a GBRf customer whose work is shared with DB Cargo. On this occasion No. 66709 *Sorrento* is in charge of a Bicester to Doncaster working consisting of a rake of empty MOD vehicle carriers and a single van on the rear.

The coal-burning power station at Ratcliffe-on-Soar, Nottinghamshire, continues to see regular coal deliveries, including GBRf workings from Immingham Docks on South Humberside. On 1 March 2017, No. 66710 *Phil Packer BRIT* heads through Mexborough on a rake of empties returning from Ratcliffe for stabling at Doncaster yard.

No. 66710 was used on a move in connection with a diesel gala on the North Norfolk Railway. On 7 June 2016, it passes Nuneaton taking Nos 50026 and 33035 from Eastleigh to Peterborough, via the Great Western Society's base at Didcot.

Several GBRf Class 66s have unique liveries, often linked to key customers. One such example is No. 66711 *Sence*, seen here at Marholm, to the north of Peterborough, on 25 April 2015. The Aggregate Industries livery recognises the importance GBRf places in handling that business's traffic from Bardon Hill Quarry, at Coalville in Leicestershire. On this occasion the loco is hauling a Southeastern EMU from its Slade Green depot near Dartford to Doncaster Wabtec works for attention.

GBRf also handles the movement of sand for Sibelco UK from Middleton Towers, near King's Lynn, to destinations in Yorkshire. On 6 April 2018, No. 66712 *Peterborough Power Signalbox* approaches Manea with a loaded service to Goole.

The downturn in GBRf coal traffic has been partly offset by the movement of biomass to the power station at Drax, in particular. On 30 May 2019, No. 66713 *Forest City* heads south through Doncaster on an empty hopper working to Liverpool Biomass Terminal for loading.

This scene on 20 July 2019 further demonstrates the geographical range now covered by GBRf. Following an overnight engineers' possession near Dumfries, No. 66714 *Cromer Lifeboat* passes Floriston crossing on the Anglo-Scottish border, returning its wagons to Carlisle Kingmoor yard.

On 3 May 2017, No. 66715 *Valour* passes the closed Barnetby East signal box on a loaded coal working from Immingham Docks to Ratcliffe power station. Colour light signalling is now the order of the day at this much-loved spotters' location.

Angerstein Wharf, Greenwich, is another destination served by GBRf-operated aggregates traffic to and from Bardon Hill Quarry in Leicestershire. On 1 December 2017, No. 66716 *Locomotive & Carriage Institution Centenary 1911–2011* approaches Clapham Junction with the return working, which snakes round London in order to reach the Midland Main Line.

The closure of Puma Energy's storage facility at Immingham heralded the end of the GBRf traffic flow between Humberside and Theale. On 10 May 2017, No. 66717 *Good Old Boy* heads north through Bedford, taking the empty tanks back to Immingham. This loco was the last numbered of the batch of Class 66s that arrived in 2003.

GBRf has a long association with the traffic to and from Network Rail's Whitemoor Yard at March in Cambridgeshire. On 10 August 2018, No. 66718 *Sir Peter Hendy CBE* passes Manea on a circular move via Ely. The train will be turned using the triangle at nearby Ely. This loco is another to carry a unique livery, one that promotes the London Transport Museum.

GBRf is one of the freight operators handling infrastructure workings out of both Hoo Junction, in Kent, and Eastleigh, near Southampton. Workings between the two yards are routed via south London. This working, on 30 June 2016, shows No. 66719 *Metro-Land* approaching Clapham Junction on one such working.

Another important hub for aggregate traffic is the Tarmac-owned quarry at Mountsorrel in Leicestershire, which is one of the largest granite quarries in Europe. GBRf operates regular services to and from the site. On 21 July 2016, No. 66720, currently unnamed, waits to couple up to its rake of wagons once loaded. This locomotive carries a unique rainbow livery.

Another unique livery has been applied to No. 66721 *Harry Beck*. It incorporates the iconic London Underground map on the loco's sides, which was designed by Harry Beck in the 1930s. In this view, taken on 23 September 2016, the loco stands at the entrance to the much-reduced yard at Hither Green in South-East London.

The daily infrastructure working from Bescot to Toton and return had been in the hands of DB Cargo going back to the early days of privatisation. It is now in the hands of GBRf. On 25 April 2019, No. 66722 *Sir Edward Watkin* is seen passing Burton-on-Trent on the Toton-bound working. This was the last of a batch of five locos which arrived via Newport Docks in April 2006. In addition to the rake of wagons, DB Cargo's Nos 66139 and 66140 are marshalled behind the GBRF loco.

The Immingham to Bedworth Puma Oil working was another latterly handled by GBRf until the terminal at Bedworth, near Nuneaton, closed in early 2018. No. 66723 *Chinook* hauls the return empty tanks through Nuneaton on 9 February 2017. At the time the loco was in the First Group's colours of dark blue, pink and white.

GBRf is one of the main beneficiaries of track improvement work on the alternative lines between Doncaster to Peterborough. The route via Lincoln offers extra freight paths between the two locations, avoiding the East Coast Main Line. These workings include the intermodal traffic between Masborough, Rotherham, and the port of Felixstowe. On 8 March 2018, No. 66724 *Drax Power Station* passes Gainsborough's Lea Road station bound for Felixstowe.

Monday morning often sees locos despatched from the company's Peterborough hub to commence weekday services. This usually includes a light engine movement to the intermodal terminal at Hams Hall in the West Midlands. On 8 January 2018, No. 66725 *Sunderland,* together with No. 66728, heads through Leicester station bound for Hams Hall. The company's founder, John Smith, is known to be a particularly keen follower of Sunderland FC's Black Cats!

Locos are also moved between the company hubs at Peterborough and Doncaster by incorporating their movements into existing wagon scheduling, particularly at weekends. On Saturday 4 July 2015, No. 66726 *Sheffield Wednesday* leads Nos 66714 and 66728 and a rake of empty sand wagons south through Marholm.

No. 66727 *Maritime One* was outshopped in Maritime Transport's house colours in recognition of the importance of the customer to GBRf. On 20 February 2018, the loco is seen heading north through King's Sutton, near Banbury, on a local Ministry of Defence working from Bicester to Kineton. This was the last numbered of the batch of five that were delivered just before Christmas 2006.

Eastleigh is an important base for GBRf locos, particularly as the company has recently taken over the main yard there. On 14 July 2018, No. 66728 *Institution of Railway Operators* is seen stabled adjacent to Eastleigh station platforms. It has Nos 66716 and 59003 for company. Locos from Nos 66728–66732 inclusive arrived in the UK in April 2008.

Another long-standing flow from Aggregate Industries' Bardon Hill Quarry sees deliveries to its plant at Tinsley, Sheffield. On 19 July 2016, No. 66729 *Derby County* heads south through Chesterfield with the returning empties.

As already mentioned, GBRf coal traffic has seen a dramatic reduction in recent years. Back in 2013, the level crossing at Hillam Gates, near Selby, was a popular location to view the coal traffic to and from the coal-burning Yorkshire power stations. In this view, on 8 June 2013, No. 66730 *Whitemoor* passes the crossing heading a rake of empty coal hoppers back to Tyne Dock.

Similarly, the lines around Doncaster station were a hub for coal movements. In a scene that's now virtually consigned to history, No. 66731 *InterhubGB* heads south through the station platform, on 17 July 2014, with a rake of hoppers for stabling at the nearby Decoy Yard.

Another GBRf flow runs between Aggregate Industries' Isle of Grain base, near Rochester in Kent, to its asphalt plant at Colnbrook, near Slough. On 5 April 2018, No. 66732 *GBRf The First Decade 1999–2009 John Smith MD* is seen passing Acton Yard on a working bound for Colnbrook.

As mentioned in the introduction to this book, No. 66732's naming came as a surprise to the company's Managing Director as he'd not expected his own name to be included! The naming ceremony at Minehead on the West Somerset Railway marked the first ten years of the company, in 2009, disproving his claim that locomotives are 'only named after dead people'!

In 2019, GBRf started handling a new gypsum flow from A. V. Dawson's Middlesbrough base to Hotchley Hill in Leicestershire, reached via a branch from the Midland Main Line at Loughborough. On 2 August 2019, No. 66733 *Cambridge PSB* approaches Chesterfield station working the return empties to the North East. The loco was one of a batch acquired from a competitor, Direct Rail Services (DRS), in 2011 and was previously numbered 66401.

Loco No. 66734 *The Eco Express*, formerly No. 66402, had a short life under GBRf ownership. On 1 December 2011, the then unnamed loco is seen passing Nuneaton on a working from Carlisle to the National Recycling Centre at Whitemoor Yard.

No. 66734 was to be named *The Eco Express* just a few weeks after the previous photo was taken. Only a few months later, in June 2012, it met an untimely end on Scotland's West Highland Line whilst working the loaded Alcan tanks, containing alumina powder, from North Blyth to Fort William. The train derailed on the shores of Loch Treig between Corrour and Tulloch following a landslip. Thankfully, the driver was unharmed. The remote location, however, meant the decision was taken to cut up the loco on site the following year.

Tarmac's quarry at Bayston Hill, Shropshire, is the start point for another aggregates flow for GBRf. The quarried stone is moved by lorry to nearby Coton Hill, where the railyard is used for loading the hoppers for onward delivery to Tinsley, Sheffield. On 31 January 2017, No. 66735 heads south through Tamworth's High Level platforms heading for Coton Hill. The loco, then unnamed, was numbered 66403 whilst with DRS.

The extent of GBRf's geographical range of freight services is evident in this working. On 13 October 2017, No. 66736 *Wolverhampton Wanderers,* formerly numbered 66404, heads south through Scotland's West Highland Line station at Crianlarich. It is working the return Alcan empties from Fort William to North Blyth on a particularly wet and uninviting morning.

On 3 October 2017, No. 66737 *Lesia* is seen heading south through Carlisle station. It is hauling a rake of empty twin flats from the nearby Kingmoor Yard to Doncaster. It was formerly numbered 66405.

Loco No. 66738 *Huddersfield Town* was the first loco of a batch of four acquired from another competitor, Freightliner Heavy Haul, in 2011. Previously numbered 66578, the loco is seen on 17 June 2015 pausing at Peterborough station whilst working an intermodal from Felixstowe to Doncaster.

Doncaster station is again the location of this coal working on 25 February 2014. Making use of a rake of open box wagons, No. 66739 *Bluebell Railway* heads south to stable its wagons in the nearby Decoy Yard. Its former Freightliner identity was No. 66579.

One of the well-established infrastructure workings links the yards at Toton and Crewe, with a return working most weekdays. On 11 February 2014, No. 66740 heads through Burton-on-Trent on the Crewe-bound train. The loco was to be named *Sarah* a few months later and was previously numbered 66580 when with Freightliner.

Two more infrastructure yards that have been linked by regular traffic moves are Hoo Junction, in Kent, and Whitemoor, near March in Cambridgeshire. On 2 April 2018, No. 66741 *Swanage Railway* heads north through Hitchin bound for Whitemoor. It was previously numbered 66581.

GBRf loco No. 66742 *ABP Port of Immingham Centenary 1912–2012* has had not one, but two, previous owners. Originally a DRS loco as No. 66406, it was subsequently acquired by Colas Rail and became No. 66841, passing to GBRf in the summer of 2011. It is seen passing over Ely level crossing on 12 October 2016 hauling an intermodal from Felixstowe.

Loco No. 66743 has had a similar past, as No. 66407 and then No. 66842. Although unnamed, this loco now carries a Belmond Royal Scotsman livery. Usually employed on these passenger duties, it is seen on an intermodal service, on 14 December 2018, pausing at Peterborough whilst working from Felixstowe to Birch Coppice.

Loco No. 66744 was the third in this batch, previously numbered 66408 and 66843. It had been renumbered by the time this photo was taken on 16 November 2011. Still sporting its Colas colours, it heads north through Nuneaton whilst dragging Pendolino No. 390055, on delivery to Alstom's depot at Longsight in Manchester. The loco has since been named *Crossrail*.

GBRf has only a handful of workings in Wales, where DB Cargo still handles the majority of traffic. The stone flow from Pengam, near Cardiff, to Neath Abbey Wharf, near Swansea, has been in GBRf's hands for many years. On 17 September 2019, No. 66745 *Modern Railways the First 50 Years*, formerly No. 66409 and then No. 66844, approaches Cardiff Central station on the westbound working to Neath.

The final loco of the batch of five moving from DRS, and then Colas, to GBRf was No. 66746, carrying Nos 66410 and 66845 previously. This loco, like No. 66743, is unnamed but also carries the Belmond Royal Scotsman colours. It is seen at Glasgow Central on the evening of 15 October 2017, waiting to remove the empty coaching stock from the terminus.

GBRf took over the haulage contract of these Belmond Ltd luxury passenger trains at the start of the 2016 tourist season, with both Nos 66743 and 66746 rebranded at this time, including the company name on the locos' bodysides. Although the season's itinerary features the whole of the UK, they are chiefly operating in Scotland.

Just before Christmas 2012, three locos, Nos 66747 to 66749, arrived in the UK from the Netherlands, via the Channel Tunnel. The first of these, No. 66747, is seen at Didcot Parkway on 30 April 2016 whilst working 'The Pines Express' railtour from Manchester Piccadilly to Eastleigh.

The loco was to be outshopped in a unique livery in July 2019 and named *Made in Sheffield*. It now carries Newell & Wright Transport livery. The company's logistics base is at Masborough, Rotherham. The loco is seen in its new guise whilst passing Melton Mowbray working Whitemoor to Mountsorrel.

GBRf has a major infrastructure yard at Wellingborough, on the Midland Main Line. In this view on 4 August 2019, a variety of wagons are on display with No. 66748 *West Burton 50* in the foreground, stabled for the weekend.

The third loco in this batch, No. 66749, remains unnamed. It is seen on 11 July 2019 as it passes Acton Yard with the return empty vans from Tilbury to Trostre, near Llanelli. The loaded eastbound working contains tinplate for the docks.

GBRf's share of the freight traffic at the southern end of the Midland Main Line continues to grow. On 12 May 2017, No. 66750 *Bristol Panel Signal Box* heads north through Bedford with a rake of box wagons from Elstow, which will stable at the company's Wellingborough Yard until their next duty. The loco arrived in the UK, via the Channel Tunnel, in June 2013 after working in Germany.

In 2014, GBRf won the contract for car traffic movements between Ford's plants at Dagenham and Garston, Merseyside. On 14 March 2017, No. 66751 *Inspiration Delivered Hitachi Rail Europe* passes Tamworth Low Level on a northbound working. This loco followed No. 66750 through the Channel Tunnel in August 2013, having also worked in Germany.

Five more Class 66s, numbered 66752–66756 inclusive, arrived in the UK via Newport Docks in July 2014. On 18 April 2017, No. 66752 *The Hoosier State* approaches Nuneaton station with a rake of empty hoppers from Westbury for loading at the quarry at Cliffe Hill Stud Farm, near Coalville in Leicestershire.

On 29 April 2017, a Saturday, No. 66753 *EMD Roberts Road* is seen leaving Eastleigh Yard on a weekend infrastructure train bound for an engineers' possession in the Horsham area.

Light engine moves between the company's depot at Peterborough and March's Whitemoor Yard are a regular feature in the area. On 6 April 2018, No. 66754 *Northampton Saints* is seen at Three Horseshoes, near Turves in Cambridgeshire, heading for Whitemoor.

On 20 July 2017, Ely Cathedral provides the backdrop for this view of No. 66755 *Tony Berkeley OBE RFG Chairman 1997–2018*. It is waiting to follow a local passenger working as it heads for Felixstowe with an intermodal from Masborough.

On 30 August 2017, No. 66756 *Royal Corps of Signals* passes March signal box heading for Doncaster on an intermodal working from Felixstowe.

The company's expansion resulted in a further delivery of no fewer than nine new Class 66s in July 2014, numbered 66757–66765 inclusive. Once again, they arrived via Newport Docks. On 1 April 2019, No. 66757 *West Somerset Railway* is seen in Derbyshire's Hope Valley. Increased work in the Peak Forest area has resulted in light engine moves between the outbase there and the company's depot at Doncaster. The loco has just passed the signal box at Edale, which still controls semaphore signals in the area.

GBRf handles the rail traffic destined for Caledonian Paper at Irvine in Ayrshire. The trains now originate from Antwerp in Belgium and convey Brazilian clay for the customer, with the working laying over in Wembley Yard after arriving in the UK. The northbound working is passing Floriston, close to the Scottish border, on 18 October 2017. The loco is No. 66758 *The Pavior*.

Another regular flow for GBRf client Aggregate Industries is that from Bardon Hill to Neasden, in North West London. This traffic operates via the Midland Main Line. On 7 October 2015, No. 66759 *Chippy* passes Bedford while returning the empty wagons to Bardon.

GBRf also operates stone traffic between Swinden Quarry, near the Yorkshire village of Rylstone, and Wellingborough. On 28 June 2018, No. 66760 *David Gordon Harris* heads north through Doncaster with a rake bound for the quarry.

The Ironbridge 'B' power station ceased to generate electricity a few months after this photo was taken. On 27 March 2015, No. 66761, unnamed at the time but now named *Wensleydale Railway Association 25 Years 1990–2015*, takes a rake of empty hoppers from the power station to the holding sidings at Tuebrook in Liverpool.

GBRf has recently added the London Gateway to Hams Hall container working to its regular weekday intermodal service schedule. Operating from DP World's complex close to the Thames at Stanford-le-Hope, the train operates to the West Midlands terminal via the North London and West Coast Main Lines. On 7 September 2017, an unnamed No. 66762 passes Milton Keynes Central on the northbound working.

On 14 July 2017, No. 66763 *Severn Valley Railway* passes Peterborough on an infrastructure working from Whitemoor to Mountsorrel for loading at Tarmac's quarry there.

Another GBRf working sees a daily return working between Tarmac's Swinden Quarry, near Rylstone, and Dairycoates, Hull. On 9 March 2016, an extremely wet day, No. 66764 passes through Leeds station with the Rylstone-bound train.

Haughley Junction, north of Stowmarket, is one of the bottlenecks that will only get busier as traffic to and from Felixstowe increases. The line used by GBRf traffic to reach Peterborough and beyond diverges from the main London to Norwich line here. On 8 September 2017, No. 66765 negotiates the junction on a Masborough to Felixstowe working.

On 6 April 2018, No. 66766 has taken the same route across East Anglia. It is seen approaching Manea on a Felixstowe to Doncaster intermodal. This loco was the first of a batch of seven Class 66s, numbered 66766–66772 inclusive, delivered via Newport Docks in early December 2014.

A GBRf freight service sees imported gypsum transported to Mountfield, near Robertsbridge in East Sussex. This traffic is brought by rail from Southampton Western Docks. On 27 April 2017, No. 66767 approaches Clapham Junction on a rake of wagons heading to the docks.

Since the company's formation, Peterborough has been an important hub for its activities, and its depot there has become a familiar sight for passengers passing on the East Coast Main Line. On 23 March 2017, No. 66768, with No. 66701 for company, is seen stabled outside the small maintenance depot.

Harrowden Junction, north of Wellingborough, is the location in this view of No. 66769 on 2 November 2017. It is working from Colnbrook to Bardon Hill. GBRf will not be directly affected by electrification of the Midland Main Line but will definitely benefit from the reinstatement of a four-track railway in the area.

Similarly, the company will be one of the major beneficiaries of the much-needed double-tracking of the branch line from Ipswich to Felixstowe. On 7 September 2017, No. 66770 passes the branch line station at Westerfield at the start of its journey from Felixstowe to Hams Hall.

On 27 April 2019, No. 66771, since named *Amanda,* is seen departing Eastleigh Yard on a weekend engineers' train. The train was heading for a line blockage in the Horsham area. This working left a few hours earlier than No. 66753, featured earlier in this publication.

On 20 February 2018, No. 66772, since named *Maria*, heads north through King's Sutton, near Banbury. The wagons are being taken for loading at Tarmac's quarry at Mountsorrel and will then be taken to Eastleigh.

The infrastructure yard at Hoo Junction, near Higham, in Kent, was home to No. 66773, seen along with No. 66777 and DB Cargo's No. 66131 on 14 December 2017. The loco has since been named *Pride of GB Railfreight* and been adorned with the rainbow colours at this year's Brighton Pride event. This loco was the first of a further seven locos, numbered 66773–66779, which arrived in the country, again via Newport Docks, in mid-February 2016.

On 21 September 2017, unnamed No. 66774 is seen heading south through Chesterfield. It is on an infrastructure working that sees regular wagon exchanges between the yards at Doncaster and Toton.

As already mentioned, seven locos arrived at Newport Docks in February 2016. The locos were then worked as a single convoy from there to the company's depot at Doncaster. No. 66775, since named *HMS Argyll*, is seen here on the rear of the convoy as it has a short layover in Worcester Yard.

GBRf has recently announced that the Up Yard at March, in Cambridgeshire, is to be returned to use for wagon stabling. The Down side of the yard is also in use for wagon maintenance work. On 25 April 2019, No. 66776 *Joanne* passes through Leicester station with a short rake of wagons from Wellingborough Yard destined for March.

Another freight flow that was in the hands of DB Cargo for many years was the stone traffic from Peak Forest to Selby. Now handled by GBRf, No. 66777 *Annette* passes Doncaster on the goods line on 28 June 2018.

On 3 April 2019, No. 66778 *Darius Cheskin* is also engaged on Derbyshire stone traffic. It is seen waiting to leave Peak Forest on another loaded working.

The seven-loco convoy that arrived at Newport in February 2016 included No. 66779. The loco was delivered with its body literally under wraps. Its livery, and the name *Evening Star*, was unveiled shortly after. The loco was then put on display in York's Railway Museum. This photo was taken on 18 May that year.

By 1 March 2017, No. 66779 had several months' use under its belt when seen at Peterborough. It is passing through the station on a Felixstowe to Doncaster intermodal.

The quest for yet more Class 66s resulted in the acquisition of ten locos from DB Cargo in September 2018. These were subsequently numbered from 66780 to 66789 inclusive. Formerly numbered 66008, No. 66780 was subsequently re-liveried in the colours of key customer Cemex and named *The Cemex Express*. It is seen heading through Nuneaton on the rear of a light engine convoy to Hams Hall.

The former No. 66016, now unnamed No. 66781 as a GBRf loco, is seen here at Doncaster on 30 May 2019. It is on a Tees Dock to Doncaster intermodal working.

No. 66782, also unnamed, formerly DB Cargo No. 66046, now carries promotional branding for GBRf Charity Railtours. It is working the return empties from Bletchley to Peak Forest, unusually returning via the West Coast Main Line and seen here at Rugby.

When No. 66783, formerly No. 66058, was seen at Doncaster on 28 March 2018, it was en route to York for its covered nameplates to be unveiled. It was named *The Flying Dustman* later in the day. It had already been given its striking orange livery with Biffa branding on its bodysides.

The colourful machine is seen again on 7 May 2019. It was diagrammed for the Dagenham to Garston car train, seen northbound through Nuneaton.

On 11 June 2018, No. 66784 was a couple of weeks away from its naming as *Keighley & Worth Valley Railway 1968–2018*. The former No. 66081 is seen passing Nuneaton on the Eastleigh to Mountsorrel empty hopper working.

Formerly numbered 66132, GBRf's No. 66785 joined the company fleet in time to haul at least one coal train! On 18 October 2018, it is seen heading through Lincoln on an Immingham to Ratcliffe working.

On 31 July 2019, former DB Cargo No. 66141, now numbered 66786, is at the head of a loaded infrastructure working from Cliffe Hill Stud Farm to Bescot Yard, West Midlands.

Infrastructure work was also allocated to No. 66787, formerly numbered 66184, on 2 August 2019. On that date, it is seen passing Mexborough whilst working from Toton to Doncaster.

Previously numbered 66238 when owned by DB Cargo, No. 66788 is seen passing Edale on 1 April 2019, heading a rake of empty hoppers from Washwood Heath, in Birmingham, back to Peak Forest. This was another working that was in the hands of DB Cargo for many years. The loco has recently been named *Locomotion 15*. The naming was in recognition of the fifteenth anniversary of Locomotion museum at Shildon in County Durham.

The former No. 66250, now numbered 66789 and named *British Rail 1948–1997*, is now in BR large logo blue livery. It is seen on 21 July 2018, passing Hitchin on a Southeastern EMU move from Slade Green to Doncaster. Three further Class 66s, numbered 66790–66792, are in the GBRf pipeline, with the first two presently at Electro Motive at Longport.

## Class 73 Locomotives

As of September 2019, records show that GBRf has twenty-three Class 73s on its books. Their status varies from active through to stored, as seen in the examples that follow. One stored example is No. 73101 *The Royal Alex*', which was bought from LORAM in 2018. It is seen here at LORAM's Derby base on 10 March 2017.

The Class 73 locos date from the 1960s and some members have therefore notched up half a century of service on the UK railways. Many of them were featured in my earlier Amberley publication, *50 Not Out*. Built in 1965, No. 73107 *Tracy* is seen passing Nuneaton in a convoy of locos returning to GBRf's base at Tonbridge. They had just attended the Severn Valley Railway, Kidderminster.

Several examples are usually found at the company's Tonbridge base. On 14 December 2017, No. 73109 is stabled in the yard between duties.

On the same day, No. 73119 *Borough of Eastleigh* is also seen in Tonbridge Yard. These electro-diesels are synonymous with the former Southern Region, with several locos continuing to carry names that recognise this.

The class duties include infrastructure work, particularly during the leaf fall season and periods of icy weather. On 14 December 2017, No. 73128 *OVS Bulleid CBE Southern Railway* is seen leaving the yard, along with No. 73141, on one such duty.

The Class 73s are also used on more general Network Rail duties, particularly on the former Southern Region. On 7 May 2015, No. 73136 is seen approaching Clapham Junction with classmate No. 73128 on the rear.

No. 73139 was also bought from LORAM in 2018 and, along with No. 73101, is believed to be stored at Eastleigh. It is seen, sporting LORAM's promotional livery, at Derby on 10 March 2017.

The Class 73s are also regularly stabled at Eastleigh. On 29 April 2017, No. 73141 *Charlotte* is stabled outside the former workshops there between duties.

Other examples of Class 73s operated under the Gatwick Express franchise, with renumbering to sub-Class 73/2 to differentiate. A number of these machines are now in use with GBRf. On 8 May 2013, No. 73201 *Broadlands* approaches London Bridge on another Network Rail Test Train, with No. 73107 on the rear.

From time to time the class can be seen away from its usual Southern Region area, often making return trips to Derby. One such example is seen on 13 October 2015 with No. 73212 on the rear of a Tonbridge to Derby service as it passes Market Harborough.

Classmate No. 73213 *Rhodalyn* is on more familiar territory on 14 July 2014. It is seen stabled at Eastleigh on the lines adjacent to the station platforms.

A further sub-series of the class was created by GBRf with five locos, Nos 73961–73965, allocated to Network Rail duties. No. 73961 *Alison* was on empty coaching stock on 15 July 2018 when leading No. 73963 on a Peterborough to Eastleigh move, seen approaching its destination.

On 24 May 2016, No. 73962 *Dick Mabbutt* was on its more usual duties. It is seen approaching Leicester on a Network Rail working from Derby to Tonbridge.

No. 73963 *Janice* was leading No. 73961 in this second Eastleigh view of this charter. On 14 July 2018, the day before the previous shot, the pair are working the Weymouth to Stevenage return.

With No. 73964 *Jeanette* nearest the camera, it's unusual to see four of this sub-class in one convoy. The other three locos are Nos 73961, 73962 and 73963. They are seen heading north from Bedford on 11 June 2015, on a move from Tonbridge to the Brush workshops at Loughborough.

The class are also occasional visitors to GBRf's depot at Peterborough. On 24 February 2016, No. 73965 is stabled there, with a more usual Class 66 occupant for company.

The final sub-series of Class 73s contains locos numbered 73966–73971. These are specifically allocated to Caledonian Sleeper duties. At the time of writing, these duties are chiefly the Highland Sleeper services to both Aberdeen and Fort William, to and from Edinburgh Waverley. On 25 October 2017, No. 73966 is seen in a light engine convoy passing Conisbrough. The loco is returning to Craigentinny depot, Edinburgh, from Loughborough's Brush workshops.

On 3 November 2015, No. 73967 was an occupant of those workshops at Loughborough. The company has almost completely rebuilt these six locos for these specific services.

The small stabling point at Fort William is the location of this shot of No. 73968 on 4 November 2018. The loco had spent the weekend there.

On the opposite side of Scotland, No. 73969 has just arrived at Aberdeen on 26 October 2018. It is in the process of running around the now empty coaching stock for movement to nearby Ferryhill for servicing.

On 6 November 2018, No. 73970 is seen around daybreak whilst calling at the West Highland station at Crianlarich. It is waiting time before continuing the two-hour journey from here to Fort William.

Another long-distance light engine move on 19 April 2017 involved No. 73971. It is seen passing Chesterfield on a Craigentinny to Loughborough move.

# Class 86 & Class 87 Locomotives

## Class 86

Two Class 86 electric locos are in use with GBRf, usually deployed on sleeper coaching stock and connected light engine moves. On 8 April 2019, No. 86101 *Sir William A Stanier FRS* is seen heading south through Nuneaton on a light engine move. It is being dragged by No. 92014 from Crewe to Wembley.

The second Class 86 is fellow veteran No. 86401 *Mons Meg*. It is seen at Glasgow Central on 9 November 2018. It is about to haul the empty coaching stock which has arrived on the Glasgow portion of the Lowland Sleeper. The stock will be moved to nearby Polmadie depot for servicing.

## Class 87

Also used on these duties is No. 87002 *Royal Sovereign*. It is seen passing Marholm, north of Peterborough, on 9 January 2019 whilst working light engine from Willesden to Doncaster.

This loco is the only mainline-registered Class 87 left in service. It was also at Peterborough on East Coast Main Line action on 6 March 2015. The Class 87 was dragging Nos 92018 and 92033, southbound this time, on a Doncaster to Willesden move.

## Class 92 Locomotives

GBRf has sixteen Class 92 locos on its books, of which four are long-term stored (Nos 92021, 92040, 92045 and 92046), leaving twelve operational. The last of these to be made available was No. 92006. This loco finally emerged from Brush's workshops at Loughborough in July 2019. It is seen being dragged through Nuneaton by No. 66704, heading for Crewe. The loco had been out of traffic since being stored back in 2006.

The locos see limited use on freight traffic these days. They do, however, appear on the Ford car traffic between Dagenham and Garston. On 8 March 2016, No. 92010 is seen through Nuneaton on a northbound service.

These locos are now finding regular use on the Lowland Sleeper services linking London with Edinburgh and Glasgow, using recently delivered Mk 5 stock. Caught between duties, No. 92014 is seen alongside the wall at Edinburgh Waverley station on 6 October 2017.

The empty sleeper stock from the Edinburgh portion of the service is worked across to Polmadie depot, Glasgow, for servicing. On 24 October 2018, No. 92018 is in charge as it heads through Haymarket.

Associated light engine moves are a necessity for servicing purposes. On 15 April 2019, No. 92020 and Freightliner's No. 90049 are seen heading north through Nuneaton, working from Wembley to Crewe.

A less common light engine working on 13 March 2017 saw No. 92023 being dragged through Leicester by No. 73961 on a Tonbridge to Loughborough Brush move.

Still sporting its previous Europorte colours, and *Saint Saens* name, No. 92028 arrives at Glasgow Central on 9 April 2015 with that city's portion of the sleeper from London Euston. It was shortly to visit the works to receive its Caledonian Sleeper livery.

Europorte-liveried No. 92032 is seen heading south through Milton Keynes Central on 12 March 2015. The loco is working from Daventry to Dollands Moor.

On 23 February 2015, No. 92033 is seen at Crewe. It had just arrived in the bay platform here whilst out on a test run to Stafford and back.

On the evening of 6 November 2018, No. 92038 arrives at Glasgow Central with sleeper stock from Polmadie depot. The coaches will later form the Glasgow portion of the London Euston-bound Lowland Sleeper.

Another light engine move featured No. 92043 on 21 March 2016. It is seen here passing Stafford on a Crewe to Willesden move. The loco now has GBRF livery and has lost its former name, *Debussy*.

Likewise, No. 92044 has been re-liveried since this photo was taken. It is seen on the wet morning of 26 November 2014 stabled in the south bay at Rugby station. It has also since had its name, *Couperin*, removed.

## GBRf Shunters

GBRf's recent takeover of yards, such as Eastleigh and Bescot, has seen a welcome return for the diesel shunter. For example, No. 08511 is one of those hired in for use at Eastleigh. It is seen there on 21 August 2019 at work in the east yard.

## A Selection of Wagons in use by GBRf

In addition to the growing loco fleet, GBRf has a fleet of more than 1,000 wagons on its books, as well as those owned or leased by its customers. A few examples of both are featured on the next few pages. A number of HTA hoppers, formerly used by DB Cargo on coal traffic, have been acquired. These include No. 310370, seen here at Peak Forest, now used in a rake of aggregate wagons.

GBRf's own pool of HYA hoppers were also used on coal traffic. Now rebranded, No. 371015 carries a variety of vinyls as it passes through Chesterfield, also on an aggregate working.

A small fleet of Bogie Ballast Hopper Wagons, designated HQAs and numbered 380701–380710 inclusive, was jointly branded with GBRF and Metronet vinyls. No. 380704 is seen here in Hinksey Yard, near Oxford.

A variety of box wagons are on GBRf's books; these include a pool of MJAs, once operated by Freightliner. Now sporting Europorte livery, No. 502050 is seen at Doncaster.

A number of bogie aggregate wagons are in general use, chiefly on infrastructure workings. This example, No. 503050, stands in Doncaster's West Yard still sporting GBRf early branding and the 'renewing the tube' message.

GBRf's fleet of FEA container twin wagons find use on various workings. For example, No. 640681 is seen here at Clapham Junction in a rake of gypsum containers heading for Southampton.

By contrast, No. 640906, in its distinctive yellow livery, is amongst a general infrastructure rake seen at Burton-on-Trent on the GBRf-hauled Bescot to Toton working.

Some of the earliest wagons used on GBRf container traffic date back to 2003. A batch of around fifty FEAs, including No. 650041, seen here at Doncaster, are still in use today, with this example currently working from Trafford Park to Felixstowe.

In 2017, GBRf leased forty-one new IIA hoppers for the sand flow the company operates on behalf of Sibelco, King's Lynn. One of these, No. 7006590316, is seen passing Manea.

GBRf is an important player in the movement of pelletised biomass from our UK ports. One of the IIA covered hoppers, designed specifically for Drax for this purpose, is seen at Barnetby. It is numbered 7006980796 and has a capacity of 70 tons.

On its intermodal trains, GBRf has a pool of Ecofret triple container wagons, which allow the minimisation of empty spaces within their trains. An example of this is seen at Nuneaton, with FWA No. 7045201352 nearest the camera.

GBRf uses a large pool of open bogie box wagons for a variety of products, including aggregates. Appropriately GBRf branded, JNA No. 7055004748 is seen at Doncaster.

GBRf intermodal services also utilise IKA Megafrets. These are low-platform twin sets such as this example, No. 8049091523, seen here at Leicester in pristine condition.

For me, the company's prospects for a bright future are summed up in this final photo. A convoy of seven newly arrived Class 66s pause in Worcester Yard on 1 February 2016. No. 66708 is towing; No. 66775 is nearest the camera and No. 66779 is still under wraps. Just as significant for me was the enthusiasm demonstrated by the accompanying train crew as they chatted to the gathered crowd of enthusiasts at the other end of the platform. I felt exactly the same on the night that the two Class 50s were unleashed at Eastleigh in March 2019. Well done, GBRf!